Dinosaur Digs

Discovering Pteranodon

Written by Rena Korb
Illustrated by Ted Dawson

Content Consultant:
Kenneth Carpenter
Curator of Lower Vertebrate Paleontology & Chief Preparator
Denver Museum of Nature and Science

magic Wagon

visit us at www.abdopublishing.com

Published by Magic Wagon, a division of the ABDO Publishing Group, 8000 West 78th Street, Edina, Minnesota 55439.
Copyright © 2008 by Abdo Consulting Group, Inc. International copyrights reserved in all countries. All rights reserved.
No part of this book may be reproduced in any form without written permission from the publisher.

Looking Glass Library™ is a trademark and logo of Magic Wagon.

Printed in the United States.

Text by Rena Korb
Illustrations by Ted Dawson
Edited by Jill Sherman
Interior layout and design by Emily Love
Cover design by Emily Love

Library of Congress Cataloging-in-Publication Data
Korb, Rena B.
  Discovering Pteranodon / Rena Korb ; illustrated by Ted Dawson ; content consultant, Kenneth Carpenter.
     p. cm. — (Dinosaur digs)
  ISBN 978-1-60270-108-3
  1. Pteranodon—Juvenile literature. I. Dawson, Ted, 1966- ill. II.
Title.
QE862.P7K67 2008
567.918—dc22
                              2007034069

FOSSIL FINDS

Professor Othniel C. Marsh found the first *Pteranodon* (tuh-RA-nuh-dahn) fossil in 1870. He had led a fossil-hunting trip through Nebraska, Colorado, and Kansas. On one of the last days of the trip, Marsh came across a bone in the Smoky Hill Chalk of Kansas. He marked the spot with a cross and took the fossil home with him.

The fossil showed a bone that was six inches (15 cm) long and one inch (3 cm) wide. Marsh thought the bone was similar to the bone of a pterodactyl, a flying reptile that had lived in Europe. But this bone was much larger.

The next year, Marsh returned to the Smoky Hill Chalk. When he found more bones belonging to the fossil, he made a surprising discovery. The bones belonged to a new type of pterodactyl. He called it *Pteranodon*.

For as long he could remember, Hong had loved dinosaurs and other ancient animals. He learned about dinosaurs from books and the Internet. He also learned from his father, a paleontologist. Even though he was only nine years old, Hong had already traveled around the world to hunt for fossils.

For this trip, Hong had traveled to the Smoky Hill Chalk in Kansas. The truck bounced along with Hong's father at the wheel and Hong and his friend Sarah in the backseat. Hong looked forward to sharing his hobby with Sarah and helping her on her first dig.

The truck passed jagged yellow and orange cliffs, but in Hong's mind, a sea covered the land. Waves rolled as huge sea creatures swam through the ocean. Above their heads flew strange-looking giant reptiles.

"What kind of dinosaurs do you think we'll find?" asked Sarah, bringing Hong out of his daydream.

"This used to be a giant sea, so there probably won't be any dinosaur fossils. Dinosaurs only lived on land," Hong explained. "Maybe we'll find fossils of fish or sharks or even sea turtles as big as a small car. Flying reptiles like the *Pteranodon* used to live here, too."

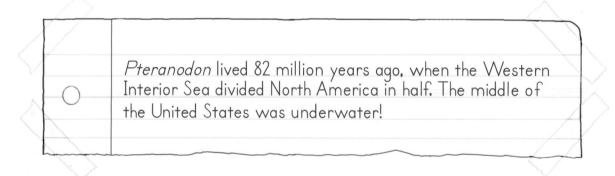

Pteranodon lived 82 million years ago, when the Western Interior Sea divided North America in half. The middle of the United States was underwater!

"*Pteranodon* had a huge wingspan," Hong said, stretching his arms wide. "They measured 25 feet from the tip of one wing to the other. That's almost eight meters long! They soared over the ocean, swooping down from the sky to snatch fish for dinner."

"I'm glad they're not still around," laughed Sarah. "They're so big, they might grab us!"

Pteranodon belonged to a group of animals called pterosaurs. Pterosaurs were flying reptiles that lived at the same time as the dinosaurs, but they were not dinosaurs.

The next day, the sun shone bright and hot. Hong, his father, and Sarah wound in and out of rocks shaped like towers and castles. They hiked along the base of tall cliffs, picking up small rocks and stepping around short shrubs.

Bones can appear when wind and water carry away the rock on the face of a cliff. Eventually, a fossil hunter like Hong might come by and spot a bone that has been uncovered.

But at the end of the day, the group had still not found any fossils.

"Don't give up," Hong told Sarah after they returned to their campsite. "Hope is one of a fossil hunter's best tools."

The next morning, the fossil hunters headed east instead of west. The day seemed even hotter than the one before, but Hong was hopeful. He did not want Sarah to go home empty-handed on her first trip!

And then, Hong noticed something sticking right out of the cliff face. He ran over. "Dad! Sarah! Come quick!"

The object looked a bit like the end of a stick, but it was blue-gray, not brown.

"This sure looks like a bone," Hong said slowly. "But fossil bones are usually brown. . . . The sunlight must have faded it."

"What's the bone from?" Sarah asked.

"I don't know," Hong smiled. "I guess we'll have to dig to find out."

Hong had brought extra gear for Sarah. From his backpack he pulled out goggles and gloves. "We have to use these to protect our eyes and hands from sharp rocks," he explained, tapping his goggles with his knuckles.

The rock of the Smoky Hill Chalk in Kansas is actually made of tiny fossils! Chalk is a type of rock that is formed mostly from the shells of tiny sea creatures called plankton.

16

Then, Hong and his father got started with their chisels. The sharp tools chipped away at the rock around the fossil. After watching them carefully, Sarah took a turn. Hong thought she held the chisel like a natural fossil hunter.

It took a lot of hard work and a lot of sweat, but they removed enough rock to see the rest of the bone. It was long—almost two feet (.6 m) by Hong's tape measure—and thin. Hong had never seen any bone like it.

"What is it, Dad?" he asked.

"You tell me," Hong's father replied.

Hong stared up at the sky. As he thought, he saw a bird swoop through the air.

"I've got it!" he cried. "It's from a *Pteranodon*."

"That's right," said Hong's father. "This is a finger bone. *Pteranodon* had three small fingers. The fourth finger was much longer, long enough to support the wing."

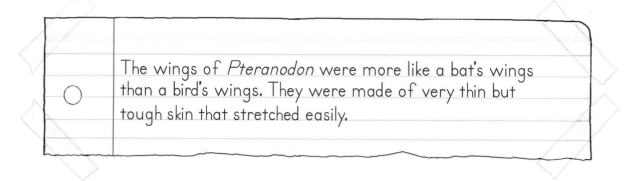

The wings of *Pteranodon* were more like a bat's wings than a bird's wings. They were made of very thin but tough skin that stretched easily.

Hong and Sarah returned to work, chisels chipping away at the cliff. While they worked, they talked about the *Pteranodon*. Sarah asked how *Pteranodon* could fly when they were so large.

Hong explained, "*Pteranodon* had hollow bones. Even though their bodies were large, they were not heavy. A full-grown *Pteranodon* only weighed as much as a two-year-old."

Hong's father added, "*Pteranodon* also used the warm air to help them soar over the water. Warm air rises in the sky, and *Pteranodon* rose with it."

All the while, the group kept digging. But by the time the sun was setting, they had not found anything more. They tied a red handkerchief to a shrub near the cliff, so they could find their way back to the site. Then, they headed to camp for a good night's sleep.

The next day, a group of paleontologists from a nearby museum met them at their campsite. This time, they drove the truck out to the dig site. If they got lucky, they would have a wonderful fossil to give to the museum.

They dug for so long that Hong almost worried they would not find anything else. "Keep hoping," he reminded himself. Suddenly, Hong's father gave a yell of victory. He had found more bones!

With growing excitement, Hong showed Sarah how to use a brush to sweep away the dirt and tiny bits of rock. The shape of the *Pteranodon* began to appear. *Pteranodon* had a large head and huge wings but a small body. Sarah was surprised to see its head was almost twice the length of its body.

They uncovered the jawbone, which stretched several feet long. *Pteranodon* did not have teeth, but one look and Hong understood how easy it would be for *Pteranodon* to scoop fish out of the ocean.

Hong and Sarah brushed away dirt to reveal a long bone angling backward from the back of the skull. "That's its crest," Hong explained. "All *Pteranodon* had them on top of their heads."

Pteranodon crests came in different shapes. One *Pteranodon* might have a crest that looked like a pointy hat, but another's crest might look like an angel's wing.

The group found leg bones, the spine, and bones that supported the reptile's powerful wings. Through it all, Hong snapped away with his camera. He knew that a paleontologist always documents an important find with pictures.

Soon, all that was left to do was get the fossil ready to move. First, they spread thin, liquid glue over the bones to make sure they did not come loose.

Next, the adults cut blocks out of the cliff. That is the best way to move bones without disturbing them.

After wrapping the blocks in a foam jacket, the adults struggled to carry them to the car. Hong's father slammed the door of the truck closed. Just like that, they were done. For a moment, no one spoke.

Hong's voice piped up. "We've still got a few days left. What should we look for now?"

Everyone laughed.

Scientists may remove bones individually if it makes them easier to move. Then, they put the bones back together before displaying them in museums.

ACTIVITY: Tools for Digging

What does a paleontologist use these tools for?

1. goggles and gloves

2. chisel

3. small brushes

4. shovel

5. camera

6. glue

ANSWERS: 1. to protect eyes and hands from sharp rocks while hammering; 2. to cut out a block of rock that holds a fossil; 3. to remove loose dirt from bones; 4. to clear out the dirt around the bones; 5. to document an important find; 6. to hold the bones in place

GLOSSARY

chisel — a metal tool for cutting, shaping, or chipping away wood or stone.

crest — a bone growth on the top of the head of a dinosaur.

dig — a place where scientists try to recover buried objects by digging.

document — to make a record of something by writing about it or taking a picture of it.

face — the steep outer side of a cliff.

fossil — the remains of an animal or a plant from a past age, such as a skeleton or a footprint, that has been preserved in the earth or a rock.

paleontologist — (pay-lee-ahn-TAH-luh-jist) a person who studies fossils and ancient animals and plants.

wingspan — the distance from tip to tip of an aircraft's wings or of the outstretched wings of a bird or an insect.

READING LIST

Ashby, Ruth. *Pteranodon: The Life Story of a Pterosaur*. New York: N.H. Abrams, 2005.
Benton, Michael. *Flying Monsters*. London: Alligator Books, 2006.
Eldredge, Niles. *The Fossil Factory: A Kid's Guide to Digging Up Dinosaurs, Exploring Evolution, and Finding Fossils*. Lanham, MD: Roberts Rinehart Publishers, 2002.

ON THE WEB

To learn more about *Pteranodon*, visit ABDO Publishing Company on the World Wide Web at **www.abdopublishing.com**. Web sites about *Pteranodon* are featured on our Book Links page. These links are routinely monitored and updated to provide the most current information available.